# GUINNESS WORLD RECORDS

## TOP 10

**Laura Barrett, Craig Glenday, Kim Lacey, Betty Halvagi, Stuart Claxton**

## SCHOLASTIC INC.

New York  Toronto  London  Auckland  Sydney
Mexico City  New Delhi  Hong Kong  Buenos Aires

The publisher would like to thank the following for their
kind permission to use their photographs in this book:

Cover, title page: © Martin Harvey; Gallo Images/Corbis; 1: © Prenzel Photo/Animals
Animals; 2: © Royalty Free/ CORBIS; 3: © Barbara VonHoffmann/Animals Animals;
4: © Peter Arnold, Inc.; 5: © University of Michigan Museum of Zoology; 6, 11: © David A.
Northcott/CORBIS; 7: © Belinda Wright/DRK PHOTO; 8 (top): © Joe McDonald/CORBIS;
8 (bottom): © MC DONALD WILDLIFE PHOTOG./Animals Animals; 9: © Eric Zamora/IFAS/
University of Florida/AP Wide World Photos; 10: © Tim Flach/Stone/Getty Images; 12:
© PREMAPHOTOS/Animals Animals; 13: © Scott Bauer, USDA ARS, www.forestryimages.org;
14: © Scott Camazine/Photo Researchers, Inc.; 15: © Paul Sutherland/SeaPics.com; 16 (top):
© Barbara Strnadova/Photo Researchers, Inc.; 16 (bottom), 26: © Mark Moffett/Minden Pictures;
17: © Erwin & Peggy Bauer/Animals Animals; 18: © D. Heuclin/Peter Arnold, Inc.; 19: © Steve
Reekie (NZ); 20: © Brandon D. Cole/CORBIS; 21: © truk and Dr. Katherine Lambert-Pennington;
22: © Denis Scott/CORBIS; 23: © Martin Wendler/Photo Researchers, Inc.; 24: © Dr. Paul A. Zahl/
Photo Researchers, Inc.; 25, 27: © Stephen Frink/CORBIS; 28: © Jane Burton/www.BCIUSA.com;
29: © Natacha Pisarenko/AP Wide World Photos; 30: © Tim Davis/CORBIS

Guinness World Records Limited has a very thorough accreditation system
for records verification. However, while every effort is made to ensure accuracy,
Guinness World Records Limited cannot be held responsible for any
errors contained in this work. Feedback from our readers on
any point of accuracy is always welcomed.

ISBN 0-439-79189-8

Designed by Michelle Martinez Design, Inc.
Photo Research by Els Rijper
Records from the Archives of Guinness World Records

12 11 10 9 8 7                              7 8 9 10/0

Printed in the U.S.A.

First printing, October 2005

Visit Guinness World Records at www.guinnessworldrecords.com

People study animals to learn about the world.

This *Guinness World Records*™ book puts us eye to eye with the fiercest, hungriest, and most dangerous creatures of all.

Warning: These record-breakers may make you run away and hide!

# EYE TO EYE

When you meet someone, you look into their eyes and smile. We call this *friendly behavior*. To an animal, staring into its eyes and showing teeth means you want to fight it. This is *hostile behavior*. The animal tries to hurt you before you can hurt it. Run away if these top 10 record-holders smile at you!

What would you do if a stranger walked into your home — or grabbed you? Unless your parents told you everything was okay, you might yell, bite, scratch, kick, or run away! Animals act the same way. They use claws, fangs, stingers, or spray poisons for their protection. These natural tools are called **defense mechanisms**.

The fiercest animals do not like fights. They try to keep their homes and families safe, just like we do.

# Most Dangerous Bird

The cassowary bird has more than just a scary stare (left). It stands 6 feet 6 inches high. That's as tall as a basketball player! This bird is too big to fly, so it fights. There are three species of cassowary living in New Guinea and Australia. This bird has dark feathers, except around its brightly colored neck area, or **wattle**.

The *casque* is the bony growth on this bird's head.

Its three toes have strong claws. Each foot has a deadly 5-inch-long attack spike (below).

In a fight, the cassowary bird protects itself by leaping and kicking with its feet. Its sharp claws may slash an animal or person who gets too close.

Snakes use sight and sound to say, "Go away!" A rattlesnake shakes the rattle on its tail. A cobra hisses and shows hostile behavior in a **threat pose**. It straightens out its body and almost stands up on its tail. It puffs out its neck muscles into the shape of a hood. An open hood shows a colorful pattern on the snake's back (below). Nature painted these danger signs for our safety.

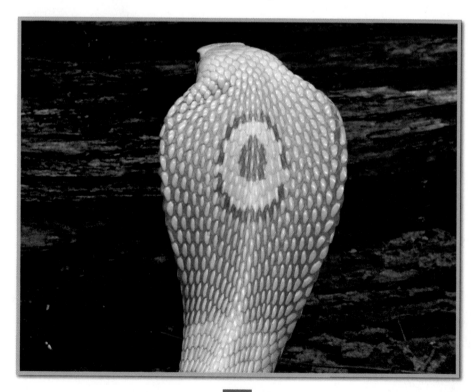

# Longest Venomous Snake

The king cobra can grow 12 to 15 feet long, about the size of your family's car. Its bite is deadly. Only 0.2 fluid ounces of its poison, or **venom**, can kill an elephant or 20 people. Combining strong poison with its awesome length, this snake is big trouble . . . but usually not for humans. The king cobra's Latin name, *Ophiophagus hannah*, means "snake eater." Other snakes are its favorite meal (left).

King cobra babies and parents have the same venom strength.

## A Good Bite

Snakes can save lives, too. Experts called snake wranglers collect the venom, or milk, from snakes in covered jars (above). The snake's fangs pierce the covering, and the fangs shoot the venom into the jar.

Doctors change this poison into medicine to cure victims of snakebites. Scientists are testing different venoms in the fight against diseases.

# A NASTY BITE

OUCH! We see a red bump. Maybe our skin itches or puffs up. Our bodies react to an animal's bite. Some animals, such as bees, *inject* poison with stingers. Other animals, such as spiders, have fangs. Watch out if these next creatures get their teeth or stingers into you. Their bites can kill.

## Most Dangerous Lizard

A Gila monster is like a small tank, growing up to 2 feet long (above). Bony plates, or **scales**, cover its large head, short legs, and thick body. This lizard moves slowly across hot, dry places in Mexico and the southwestern United States. Its body carries a secret weapon. Eight glands in its lower jaws store enough venom to kill 2 adults. If attacked, the Gila monster chews with its tiny teeth. Venom flows from its lower jaws and spills into the bite wound. The victim must find a doctor — fast!

Lizards and snakes are **reptiles**. So are turtles and crocodiles. Reptiles have back bones, breathe air, and are cold-blooded. This means they must live in sunny places to keep their bodies warm.

Lizards and snakes are closely related. Some lizards look like snakes because they do not have legs. Both use tongues to smell food. Every few months, lizards and snakes shed their dry, scaly skin. Nature painted these creatures in bright colors to show they are dangerous to others (below).

Keep watch for the largest reptile!

After a good meal, the Brazilian wandering spider looks for a place to nap (below). Its homeland is South America, but this spider has hitched a ride in a bunch of bananas going across the ocean!

At 6.75 inches, this large spider loves napping inside clothing. If awakened, it will bite. Hundreds of people report accidental bites each year. This species has the most lethal poison of any living spider. Just 0.00000021 ounces of its venom kills a mouse!

The honeybee is a stinging insect that makes honey. Special people called **beekeepers** wear protective suits when they take honey from the bees' home (above).

Bees protect their home, known as a **hive**. They attack in a group, called a **swarm**. Bees sting anyone too close to their hive until that stranger goes away.

A bee injects its stinger into your skin. The stinger carries poison into your body. Some people get very sick from a bee's poison and need to see a doctor.

The Africanized honeybee is called the "killer bee" (below). This bee is hostile. Swarms have chased people for up to a quarter of a mile.

Few people live after being attacked by a swarm. This bee's venom is the same strength as other bees. But the killer bee does not lose its stinger after the first bite. Instead, it keeps on stinging, and injecting poison, until the victim is dead. Beekeepers are working on ways to stop this angry bee from mixing in other hives.

## Most Venomous Jellyfish

Animals that sting also live in the sea. The Australian sea wasp is not a bug. It's a jellyfish, with enough poison to kill 60 humans (below)! The jellyfish is shaped like a parachute. It has many arms, called **tentacles**. Tiny poison darts, called **stinging cells**, cover each tentacle.

A person swimming near a jellyfish can be stung because chemicals on our skin set off the jellyfish's stinging cells. The Australian sea wasp's poison can kill a human within 4 minutes. Some lifeguards wear nylon pantyhose over their arms and legs to protect themselves when in the water.

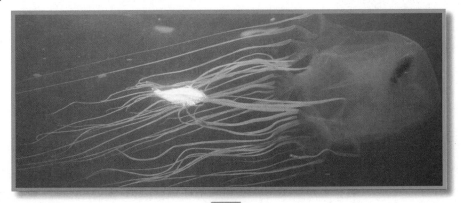

# To Bite or To Sting?

Biters use fangs to inject poison. Stingers use a barb to deliver venom.

The scorpion stings with a sharp barb at the end of its curved tail. The Most Venomous Scorpion is the Tunisian fat-tailed (above). This poisonous creature causes 90 percent of the scorpion-bite deaths in North Africa.

The bulldog ant is a biter *and* a stinger, making it the Most Dangerous Ant (below)! Its strong jaws, or mandibles, hold on while it injects venom with its stinger. Adult humans have died within 15 minutes of an attack.

This ant's bite is bad, but is it worse than a shark's bite? See page 22 for more fishy facts before you answer!

# BIG EATERS

Some animals become dangerous to humans only when they protect their homes. Others are dangerous to us all the time because they want to eat us! *Predators* are creatures that hunt, kill, and eat other animals. Any time is dinnertime for them.

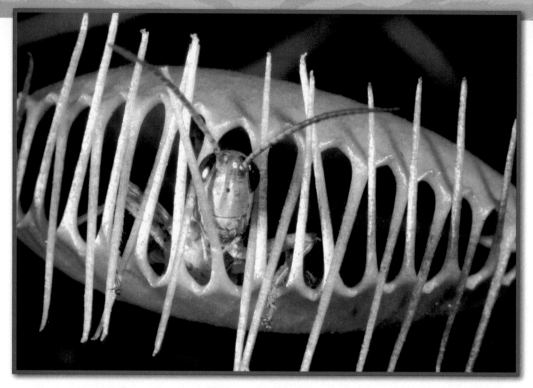

Another word for a meat eater is **carnivore**. Did you know that some plants are carnivores?

Look at the famous Venus flytrap catching a meal (above). This carnivorous plant shares the record for **Fastest Entrapment by a Plant**. An insect, like the grasshopper, walks across the plant's leaves. The Venus flytrap's clamshell-like leaves snap shut — in one tenth of a second! The bladderwort plant is the underwater record-holder. Meals fall through its hidden trapdoor and are caught in one fifth of a second.

Some plants have stingers, or **nettles**, for defense. **The Most Dangerous Stinger** belongs to New Zealand's tree nettle (below). It can grow up to 10 feet tall. Stinging hairs, like the jellyfish's stinging cells, cover its green leaves. Each hair holds many poisons. Dogs, horses, and people have died from getting too close to this plant.

More than 2,000 years ago, the Greeks named these giant reptiles after a tiny lizard called a *krokodelios*. Today, the saltwater crocodile is the **Largest Reptile** at more than 20 feet long (above and right). This predator sneaks up on its prey and uses powerful jaws to drag its meal underwater.

# Most Deaths Caused by Crocodiles

The worst attack on people by crocodiles happened during World War II. On February 19, 1945, an Imperial Japanese Army unit was stuck on the Burmese island of Ramree. Ten miles of mangrove swampland separated them from their battalion.

That night, the unit waded into the swamps. The next morning, only 20 out of 1,000 soldiers had made it to the other side. Thousands of 15-foot-long saltwater crocodiles lived in those swamps. These carnivores were hungry, and their prey walked into their home.

# Jaws vs. Claws

Do you remember the bulldog ant? The shark crushes the record for worst bite! Scientists tested the bite strength of a dusky shark. At the tip of its teeth, the shark's bite has a force of 22 tons of pressure — the same as being crushed by ten cars!

The great white shark is the Largest Predatory Fish (above). It can grow to over 15 feet long and has 3,000 teeth! This giant fish snacks more on seals and other sharks than on people. Yet, every year there are about 70 to 100 shark attacks on people worldwide, with an estimated 5 to 15 deaths.

Is a cat fiercer than a shark? Yes, if it is a man-eating cat, such as the tiger (above). The Largest Feline Carnivore has sharp claws and jaws. One cat made the record books in the early 1900s with Most People Killed by a Tiger. Scared villagers hid while a female tiger stalked Champawat, India. She ate 436 people!

Today, tigers are endangered, or in danger of dying out as a species. People building cities have taken over areas where tigers used to live. Zoos are working to save tigers from extinction.

# Most Ferocious Freshwater Fish

Drops of blood in South American river water bring this vicious fish for dinner. Piranha don't eat alone — they attack in groups of 20. A group of fish is called a **school**. They start eating right away, even if the main course is still alive! Within minutes, piranhas can turn any animal into a skeleton. They have razor-sharp teeth that fit together like puzzle pieces (below).

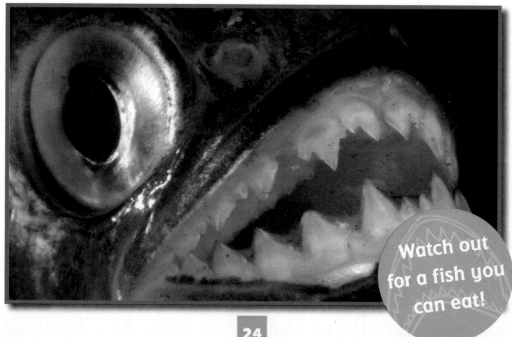

Watch out for a fish you can eat!

# HANDS OFF

We put up signs such as "Don't touch." We use strong colors to warn people to be careful. Nature did the same thing for us by painting some animals in bright colors and giving them pointy edges. These creatures are dangerous to touch or eat because even their skin is poisonous.

## Most Poisonous Frog

A simple rule about poisonous creatures is: Don't touch! This tiny frog, less than 2 inches long, makes enough venom to kill 10 people. It comes in many colors. The brightness of this animal's skin color equals the strengh of its poison. The golden dart frog is the brightest and most poisonous.

This frog of South and Central America **secretes**, or gives off, poison through its colorful skin. One drop can stop your heart.

Some hunters rub their darts on the frog's poisonous skin (below). That's why this creature is called a dart frog.

This fish could be named "spine fish" because its sharp fin spines store its poison. Instead, it is named a stonefish because it lies near the bottom of the ocean floor like a stone (above)! There are two species of this fish. One lives in Indo-Pacific waters while the other swims around the Great Barrier Reef of Australia. Both are the **Most Venomous Fish** because they have the largest venom glands of any fish. Their muddy color helps them hide among the rocks. The bright red color on their spines warns other animals not to touch them.

This fish does exactly what its name says. The puffer fish, or blowfish, of the Red Sea and the Indo-Pacific Sea sucks up water to inflate itself (above). Its scales puff out into threatening spines. Other animals stay away. Can you believe that this is a poisonous fish you can eat?

The puffer fish is a dangerous treat in Japan known as *fugu-sashi* (blowfish-raw). The fish carries a poison called **tetrodoxin** in certain organs and in its skin. You must be highly trained to prepare this dish safely, or else the person eating this meal will die within 20 minutes.

People are learning how to use nature's defenses in their own lives. We milk snakes to use their poison in curing diseases. We build special places in zoos to save the lives of tigers (below). We can better understand our world when we respect the animals living around us.

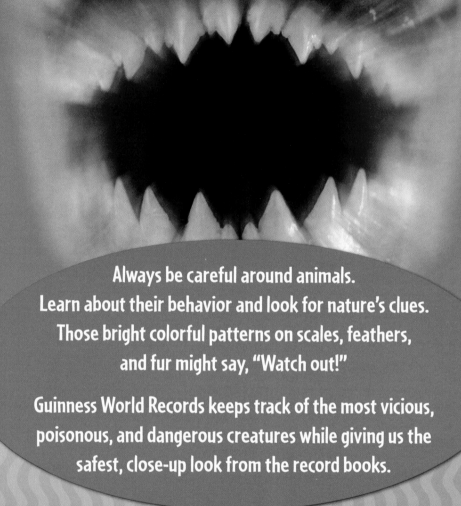

Always be careful around animals.
Learn about their behavior and look for nature's clues.
Those bright colorful patterns on scales, feathers,
and fur might say, "Watch out!"

Guinness World Records keeps track of the most vicious,
poisonous, and dangerous creatures while giving us the
safest, close-up look from the record books.